The Anthology 2026

Lost Souls Events

We are all Lost Souls until we are found.

EVENTS

ISBN-978-1-0369-6992-9

© Copyright for individual poems rests with the authors
© Anthology selection copyright: Hannah Stanislaus CF
© Logo designed by Tony Collingwood

The rights of the authors have been asserted
in accordance with the UK
Copyright, Designs and Patents Act 1988.

All rights are reserved. Without limiting the rights under the copyright reserved above, no part of this publication may be reproduced, stored in a retrieval system or transmitted in any form or by any means, electronic, mechanical, photocopying, recording or otherwise, without the prior permission of both the copyright owner and Lost Souls Events LTD.

Printed on FSC accredited paper by 4edge Limited.

This book is dedicated to all the Lost Souls we have met over the years.

The poets in this anthology mean a great deal to us.

They are the Lost Souls family.

We would love you to join our Lost Souls community.

Lostsoulsevents.com is where you can find us.

SPECIAL MENTIONS

Thank you to all those who contributed to the GoFundMe to make this anthology happen.

Thank you to those who have helped with planning and designing.

Thank you to the Higher Power who gave us all life.

Contents

Lost Souls	5
Assistance	7
Arsonist Of You	8
Apollo And Hephaetus	12
The Elephant In The Exam Hall	14
Memories Of Uncle Richard	15
My Lost Poet	19
The Hoad	20
You Snooze You Win	22
Twin Twins	24
Your Average Common Girl	26
Aches N Pains Pon A Ponderous Train	29
Finding Eden	32
That Day	33
Arsenal	34
Conspiracy Theory	36
Conversation	38
At The Alternative Disco	41
Tumblr	43
How To Grieve	44
Part Of The Act	47
The Emerald	48
Curious Furious And Sorted	49
A Moment's Quiet	51
After You, I Found Me	52
The Line	53
Her Will	56
Present In The Shade	57

LOST SOULS – Peter King

Somewhere over the horizon lies the unknown
Kingdom of the Lost Souls,
A mythical opaque quasi over crowded lone star
Slanted cacophony of writhing desires.

Pictures of Lily snuggled up to yearnings of redemption
Freedom of tension
Brain suspension
The mathematics of madness
Oily brilliance in Pandora's chest
The highest prime number possible no less
Escape from sadness
Explanations of gladness
Heaven's gate
Hell's hate
No direction from home
An eternity to roam.

We bump into each other time after time
Close the door behind us then open it up again.

Life's allotment full of ripening and decaying
The Holy men have their dry spells sowing and reaping
Never keeping

"It's just life" says Joe Public.
Taking shelter from the rain searching platonically
For an escape from pain

Brigades of the lost ones crawl deeper
into the black gaudy web to rest in silence
I write my poems dreaming of relevance shying
Away from another benevolence
After lunching
On a full stomach I look for the messenger
The essence in another
The sun out of its cover.

Blinded by the light then unfit for the fight
Tiny human ants safariing for a tinier mite

Turning up at the pearly gates with references at hand
Of crimes of the heart and worthy intentions
Or just jumbles of ignorance and the serenity
of the moon
None too soon

The moments of rest
The sky
The waves
A sacred peace when none of this striving
to make sense
Is realised as the chief offence

That's my tuppence worth.

ASSISTANCE - Zoe Fairbairns

Assisted dying? Step this way
Would you like it for today
Or will tomorrow be OK?
Click here for an up-to-date display
Of various approaches to the task
And answers to the questions you may ask.

Certain equipment will be required
But nothing that can't be bought or hired
From a garage or pet shop or DIY emporium
Or a tropical fish aquarium
Or hardware stores or pharmacies
Or sellers of sexual accessories
Or stalls for people who own a horse
Or a boat or a bike - and of course
There's that well-known high street department store
That claims to stock everything, and more.

And don't dismiss the obvious -
The contents of your attic, or something under your bed
Or lying rust-encrusted in your garden shed.
All of these can play their part
In putting a stop to the beating of your heart.

Goodbye.
Serving you has been so nice
And we hope you have been helped by our advice.
How would you like to pay the bill?
Cash or card or a clause in your Will?

ARSONIST OF YOU - Kate Griffin

You're an arsonist of you
You've made a fire out of your flesh suit
Gone hot coal walking just to see
what the world would do
I have no patience for you
Giving away our fingernails for buy-a-drink tokens
You're wearing petroleum in all of your devotions

It isn't easy to admit that you're insecure
Why have a wall there when you could have a door
But when anybody tries to walk through,
you start peeling off the paint
You splinter and lock,
see everything through a screwed-up fusion of self-hate
So you pull back, get distant

I hate you because you throw out all our convictions
When was the last time you said what you meant
and owned your predictions
You don't have to be a fortune teller to see that
your lack of boundaries have caused
your own conditions

I watch you with a splayed open chest,
With your heart in your hands
Ignoring your feelings like you're living
on someone else's plan

But nobody gets to make a blue print of you
There's a map of your life no one else in the queue

When did you let this world make you so soft
That you'd lie down with wolves and think you
were the animal
That you'd give all your time to
a corporate cannibal
Curling into something that should be
devoured by Hannibal

Look at you
Taller than a skyscraper but none of the stability
Here we go again knocking on new doors to
appease old fragility
When are you going to let you take care of you
the way you do for those lost souls you see
Aren't you just another one wandering around
denying your own capabilities

Allowing small self-robberies so you can see
what it is to confront a burglar
You're a self-murderer
Unzipping your skin to keep somebody else warm
You probably put it on a hanger,
sewed the label in your own neck,
cleaned the bed that you bled in
It is an unusual sin to forget you too are a blessing

Loving you must be disastrous disarmament
The more you think about it,
the worse you feel about the locks where your heart is
Strip away the cross bows and still you're
looking at militant bombardment
Just to know you feels like hard work and that's
why they don't want the half of it
Get a bit closer then get tired of the preview
of someone who's always giving their heart away
for fresh bread

Giving their soul away, it's not leant
Grating off your skin for the decadent
Then complaining when they ask for more
When more has always been promised in your
much too courteous outpour

I hate you for making us live like our make-up
isn't something to be won
Like we don't have a golden soul spooled
straight from the sun
Like it doesn't crawl out of our mouth to speak
beauty onto those we love
And even though we're flawed, every time it acts it tries
to do so like it's something from above

And I'm saying this to slap some sense into you
You — kicking yourself in the ribs because
somebody else's legs couldn't do it hard enough

You holding back your talents,
sure that your good enough
is just a good bluff
You need to hold my hand sometimes

You need to stop throwing us off the cliff before
we've had time to become a landmine
I'm all for going up in flames, but we're
not a dwindling match or a glum cigarette
in the hands of a mismatch
We're made to be a bit more than that

If we're going out it's in a cannon,
it's in a burst of colours,
leave the pyros in their famine
I want to be a bright light
Set alight

Bigger than sunlight
I want you to be it with me
Come, let's stop fighting
Together we can burn through the whole city

APOLLO AND HEPHAESTUS - Nadja Lima

Once, I gazed up at the flesh of you,
glistening and spent under the low sun
And deemed you marble made bone,
streaked in ichor as Gods of yore

You lacked the harshness of stone,
the tight ridges of muscle,
but I found only love in the softness,
the slow dip and descent of each curve

I traipse through museum halls,
finding your shape in every corner,
knowing not why I still return

There is a lost treasure in the crevice
where I store all you once taught me;
Ink blotted caresses and soft spoken prayers,
dissolution of vows and how rage debased Man

The ache ascribed to memory dissolves,
I am told, when strange bodies are allowed to fuse;
light that soft orange blaze and craft a new muse

I am no trueborn Hephaestus;
I choke on hot furnace air,
amble out toward colder breath
with empty hands

Was it faithless,
I question the flame,
to recall eyes unborn
when gazing at you?

I caused storms to meld with gold
and chose tempests over sunlight
Now I weep over ancient stone,
finally, an acolyte

Make a man compete with myth;
see fairly where the line glows
I am regret-woven sinew,
You are the archer, discontinued.

THE ELEPHANT IN THE EXAM HALL
Luigi Coppola

Tommy sees numbers in a sea of letters,
all shapes contorting and distorting.

Amira's hand cannot handle the pen –
its hidden river flowing up hill.

Leslie prays to The God of Questions
that they aren't asked anything ever.

Mohammad's eyes file midnight receipts
while trying to keep his head above orders.

Yirong keeps counting clouds for the trees
and scratches off the silver lining of every forest.

Tomorrow, the same dawn will rise
on the same desks, on the same tests that
Tommy, Amira, Leslie, Mohammad and Yirong
will take, all with the same elephant
(expanding and screaming and bleeding)
hanging above them, dribbling down
crosses and zeroes on every single word
they will not write.

MEMORIES OF UNCLE RICHARD - Joshua Omeke

My parents were in London for holiday
when my mother got call on a Thursday.
Uncle Richard travelled from Lagos
and was to return next Wednesday.

After a party on Friday afternoon
his legs were rocky and swollen.
The crowd whispered it was juju charms
though we pretended it was stress.

In our family we never minded about such acts
but everyone understood it dangerous potential.
Then another uncle went to his location
and transported him from Edo to Abuja.

He was admitted in a General hospital
and the doctor said the legs had poison.
They may cut his leg as the effect
was spreading faster than expected.

In desperation my mother kept sending money
to ensure he was taken care of.
By Sunday morning he was getting better.
He could sit up, eat and even sip water.

He had slept that afternoon
when a bird flew to climb his chest.
This was an omen one the elders feared and
presumed a human had come to take his heart.

In our culture birds carry warnings
sometimes missions from worlds unseen.
My other uncle tried to catch the bird
but like Icarus it flew higher and higher.

About 3am my mother received a call
he woke up shouting for no reasoning.
About 5am he was pronounced dead—
I did not cry neither did my mother.

She said her teary brook was dry from past fears.
It was either shock or acceptance of fate.
She realized she had lost her last brother—
precious loss brought her closer to feeling nothing.

We moved through the days pretending
not to be weighed by the helplessness we felt.
But what's fascinating was her change
which eventually affected us.

Death itself was a masquerade
performing unannounced.
At the time he was due for embalming
his organs were dried up in the photos.

Which looked like festers and
the mortuary attendant had an easy shift.
The sight of his withered organs left us haunted
not just by the physical decay but with questions.

In the end it didn't matter—nothing could bring him.
This part of Africa is not in the media.
The dark magic used to oppress others unaware.
His son barely cried or felt anything.

Some pain were too deep to be expressed—
following a silent celebration of promotion.
He was a police officer at the Nigerian force
and was promoted to the deputy superintendent.

At his funeral relatives said he spoke too much
and raised the wrong brows—like evil eyes.
Alas 21 gun salute proceeded
to admire his 30 years of service.

This world is harshly modelled, like—
how jealousy takes its turn on us all.
My mother became frail and uninteresting
for she had thought all the things she could.

The fading memories cleaved her senses
so she barely ate or drank but praised God.
I remember how he gave me his Glock
when he visited in my infancy to play with.

Uncle Richard's bass voice didn't just turn heads
it carried stories, jokes, and profitable wisdom.
He was tall almost imposing—
as his expectations until the enemies struck.

Uncle Richard's life and laughter lingers
a reminder of fragility in a wicked world.
Even now I hear his voice and feel his Glock
and see the wisdom in his eyes.
Perhaps he is gone, but his expectations live on
above the enemies that struck in silence."

MY LOST POET – Tim Foley

You won't know you saved my life
That your words cut like a knife
Gently pried away my skin
Peeled it back and buried in
As I watched you tug your hair
You stood and laid your life out bare
I saw my story on the stage
I ate your sorrow, drank your rage
Such a brave and stoic tale
Tore through me, a silent wail
I found my body shaking, still
Swallowed it a jagged pill
Thank you, thank you,
Jesus Christ
Have we walked through woven strife?
Cupped our hands around a light?
Shook together through the night?
What brought you here just at this time?
To comfort me with every line.
As if you'd grown up from the ground
Crept through my mind without a sound
I watched your heart float out your chest
A gift of love to help me rest
The truth that you so boldly told
I'll carry it until I'm old
I'll wear it round me when I'm cold
My fellow, pilgrim,
and lost soul.

THE HOAD – Ned Longdon

The route to the top of the lonely hill takes you
through curious patches of woodland,
over tufted fields and past coppices
that catch the very best of the Autumn light.
Keep on the path.

Resist the temptations of the bustling pubs,
where chatter runs from the taps and onto
the streets, for there is no room for you there.

Keep on the path,
now a sparsely-gravelled track,
toward the summit,
There is a bench up there, immaculately-crafted,
yet rusted, numbed by the hilltop breezes,
Take a seat.
Take a seat,
Ignore the town's lights, beneath you,
Read the long, dark sky,

Look, there is a satellite,
up there,
There's a satellite,
and you are following it along,
similarly to how you follow your pupils
in the bathroom mirror,
through the specks of starlight and smudges of cloud,
wiped away by the sleeve of the wind,

You are following the satellite,
it could be... **a million miles away**
is that where you are?
Where you want to be,
Where you'd like to stay?

No. Come back to Earth,
You may find that the town's lights, below,
have a warm, welcoming glow.

YOU SNOOZE YOU WIN – H Phillips

I wish we lived in a world where we got rewarded
for missing deadlines
getting up late
talking nonsense
sticking to our own pace

Tell me:
why must I stick to your structures and rules?
What exactly is so virtuous about
being awake
and functional
and upright?
Can't I lie around eating grape like the romans
or those whimsical women in renaissance paintings?

Missed your flight?
Congratulations
have a free upgrade

15 minutes late for work?
Automatic pay rise!

Can you tell us about a time you've
been really disorganised and missed a deadline?
Yes, I can!
Finally, I don't have to lie

Or…please, brain, can you fix your little dopamine
cogs and gears and stock up?
Not like apocalypse levels, just a bit?

Just so I can finish this one thing this
thing that opens a door to something I want
but that I also can't be bothered to do

back to bed…

I would like to actually get up and make the
most of my life really really I would
but sleepy snoozy snuggly sexy time is so
delicious

When my alarm goes off I wish my
iPhone would sprout kawaii chisai
arms and legs et un visage
'snooze me! snooze me'….
'yaaaaaay!'

That's the tenth time she's gone back to bed,
Terry incredible sleepersonship
we're seeing today
at Duvet Pillow Park

TWIN TWINS – Dennis 2

They had two twins who wrote this song
There's one named Tim and one named Tom
And one named Ping
And one named Pong
And as I said they wrote this song.

They liked to sing
They liked to pout
But mostly they would muck about
They had a dog who they would mount
And ride him til a poo fell out

It usually fell from poor Tim's bum
And once it did they all would hum
And do a dance and bury it
And ponder why it smelt like ….

They mostly would all get along
And frolic, o what could go wrong
Well Ping could pick a fight with Pong
And Tim with almost anyone

They'd play a game called 'Little War'
In which they'd punch and kick and claw
And stab and jab and spit and scratch
And terrorise all dogs and cats
And stomp on snails

Pour salt on slugs
Stick little pins in worms and bugs
And swat and swat and swat at flies
And pull the wings of butterflies.

They had two twins but never knew
Behind their backs what would ensue
And keep this just between me and you
Half of those tricks I did them too.

YOUR AVERAGE COMMON GIRL
Rebecca Nystrom

"Here's a few notes taken from my world
Kind regards and sincerely,
just your average, common girl

Who still try to find her place on this planet
Doing mainstream stuff, but still somewhat be organic

Who's trying to fit in, and at the same time be her own
Figure out what she wants, but already have it known

Who's been trying to see life from all sorts of angles,
Good girl
Bad girl
Burnt out girl
Whatever she can handle

You might think so far there's nothing odd in this blur
Could that be that after all – she is
just your average, common girl?

Who's bubbly on the outside and loves a social life
But within, the spark is long gone and she just feels empty inside

With confidence so high she knows what she brings to the table
But could you believe, at the same time, she sees herself as the definition of unstable?

With seasons on focusing on all that is bad
Questioning her sanity, if she's actually going mad

Have gone through what she would call mental abuse
Or is that just exaggeration,
to keep her life somewhat amused?

What feels like emotions stuck in a swirl
Aren't these just normal thoughts for
your average, common girl?

What is right, what is wrong, what is all this in between
Think about it all you want, just don't let it be seen

And as she can't put words on this turmoil in her head
She seeks comfort in the boys
who want to take her to bed

Who made her feel special and unique to their world
But left her with the thought - at the end,
she was just one of many girls

All she wanted to believe was
she could be loved one day
But a few ghostings and bad excuses later,
the thought started to fade

Now she's happy if she's just getting laid
Even if she would be the last choice made

Because for that one night,
 she gets to rock their world
For one night only, she's not
their average, common girl

Now reality is knocking, it's time to get back
It's time for the never ending
struggle of finding her track

Because when reality hits, she's temporarily fine
And when it starts to get unbearable,
well, at least she has her wine

The burdens she carry starts to be too many
And who would've thought all this
emptiness could be so heavy?

Hide behind fake laughs and jokes based on her pain
Empty yet sculpted, still hoping life has more to gain

Well, I hope you have enjoyed
some of these thoughts that have occurred
Kind regards and sincerely,
just your average, common girl

ACHES N PAINS PON A PONDEROUS TRAIN- KEVIN RAYMOND

Meandering… suburban train…
Body wracked in pain
Mates sit rabbiting away… about the match
Never… hurted like this before
I've sullen joints that sore
Every jolt hit home… along the winding track.

Swollen ankle… shattered ego… puffy lip
But, what really sunk… my street cred ship…
Mates had seen me crying… when I cracked
That flaming eejit… could have broke my leg?
So, when I clumped him around the head
Didn't dream… he'd have the gall… to put me on my back?

Rising up… I struck again
That hard… my right hand winced… in pain
He smashed me in the face, and on we went
Threw another right… lost my rag
A whirling banshee… wailing… mad
Rabid tears of rage… spurred on… my intent.

"You… and you… off", screamed the referee
Mates… desperate to restrain me
Tried to grab both arms… midst calming down
I caught yer man a flailing right
He replied with a left… marked… nighty night
Had it landed… I'm spark out… in La La-Town.

Looking through the mud-streaked winder
Tis a stark morning in… mid-winter
Trying to forget… those anguished tears of dread
A vivid picture… of icy dew on frosted grass
Disappears… at our carriage wobbling past
The scene…. a feckin stupid eejit… lost his head.

Back home indoors, I'm still in pain…
"Jaysus bhoy… was ye… after fighting yet again?
Hope the other fella… came off worse than ye?"
Ignoring… tears…. bruised ego, puffy lip
I make a tactical exit…
Nip out to our kitchen… stick the kettle on for tea.

"Mam! Would you like a splash o' tea?",
"Umm… everything okay bhoy, anything ta say… ta me?
Tis a rare thing… yeese making tea… without being asked?".

T'was then… I decided… not to lie…
Give my reasons why…
Or go in to the details of… how I…
The apple of… me mammy's eye…
In a fit of rage… an hour ago…
Exchanged… an array of angry blows
With a young fella… I didn't even know…
A… novice Catholic priest… hit me that hard…
I landed on me arse… on a dew-soaked playing field o' grass.

Peace... in Eastern Europe and in The Middle East.

FINDING EDEN – SIMON GARDNER

Whether we consider ourselves religious,
We are all seeking to find our own Eden,
That thing that makes us feel like we have soared up,
To far beyond the clouds and into Heaven,
All whilst remaining alive and on the ground,
As we float like in a fantasy written.

Then when we are banished from our paradise,
The ground can feel like hell in comparison,
Where we reel from our sudden falling from grace,
With it a perceived eternal sensation,
And despite this we remain on the same ground,
At the level of the last apparition.

Any external Eden is a mirage,
As our true Eden is something that's within,
We go around attributing it elsewhere,
Which causes us frequent feelings of chagrin,
Therefore, we can never be cast out from it,
That place will always remain beneath our skin.

We will find more places that feel like Eden,
And some of those will stay around as a home,
True Eden is in the heart we'll always have.

THAT DAY – DENNIS TOMLINSON

That day I was born in a storm
when an obstetrician opened his tongs,
seized and hauled my ancient head
                out of a sleeping body

into light to scream at the rain,
when Daddy paced up and down outside
and the gust tugged his black umbrella
inside-out –
                and I soared aloft

through years and years of Kubrick's space
to land at a school and walk alone
where two little boys rushed round a corner,
seized my neck
                sent me flying

                            back to the hospital.

ARSENAL – T BALOGUN

A true story
where the team
titled the underdog
becomes
The Champion.

Rene Slegers steadied the ship
with her self-belief,
determination
calmness & effective communication.

She's successfully guided Arsenal Women, who beat
Barcelona Femeni ONE: NIL, to become…

European Champions, again, starting from the first
round of
qualifying which before had never been done.

Not since 2007, has a British club (Arsenal Women)
achieved this,

A beautiful reverse pass from Beth Mead put
Stina Blackstenius through & I knew she wouldn't miss,

Leaving Lisbon as Winners, WoW, what a story!!
'cos after 18 long years, the Women of Arsenal, have
reached their goal & achieved European glory.

Winners
Once again
Motivational
European Champions 24/25
Never giving up, keeping dreams alive

CONSPIRACY THEORY – JOHN COOK

I know that you know that I know that you know
That we know that they know that nobody knows
That maybe we all know that none of us know that
She knows that he knows the world has no clothes

We think we're free or maybe
An offshore lab sets our destiny
We're all bionic electronically
Tagged and chipped from a to b

Where we go and what we do
With our time and with whom
Signals controlling us through and through
To do their bidding and keep us true

I know that you know that I know that you know
That we know that they know that nobody knows
That maybe we all know that none of us know that
She knows that he knows the world has no clothes

What if the government did it on purpose
To make it seem that the whole things a circus
Boosting their shares right up to a surplus
Or maybe it's just how it seems on the surface

Tin hats and flu jabs and 5G antennas
Taxes and axes and policy dilemmas
Thoughts that go viral creating a clamour
They're using a nut to crack a sledgehammer

I know that you know that I know that you know
That we know that they know that nobody knows
That maybe we all know that none of us know that
She knows that he knows the world has no clothes

CONVERSATION – TONY BELL

Evolution Evolution Evolution,
repeat it three times speak it with me
Evolution evolution evolution,
not bad could be better but I'll let it be

Life's one big process of Natural Selection
If you follow Darwin's "Theory of Evolution"
We're products of our parents' DNA
Like it or lump it, we're all made that way
We inherit their behaviour, their bodies, their mental health
Which they've evolved from their environment, as they've tried to help themselves
Adapt to their surroundings as all species do
It's survival of the fittest if you take Darwin's view
Fight to the death, only the strong survive
So you'd better stamp on the weak if you want to stay alive

I think that's what's happening right now in plain sight
People destroying people, in the name of what they think is right
But there are no grey areas, it's simply black or white
Kill or be killed, not live and let live
Do we really want that? Something's got to give

Can we reclaim that word that's been erased from our dictionary
That Elon Musk said is destroying his country
And Charlie Kirk claimed in tragic irony
Was a made-up New Age term that could do so much damage
Can we reclaim that word now, salvage it from the wreckage
Not "sympathy" but "empathy"- there is quite a difference
One suggests patronage at a safe distance
The other is the ability to hear another point of view
Not destroy those who speak it, if that person isn't you

The daughter of Charlie Kirk, the young man assassinated
Carries in her DNA his traits she inherited
So the memory of her father lives on in her image
Just as George Floyd lives in the daughter of his lineage
Who said in her statement how they played together all day long
And through both these daughters their parents' lives live on
Despite being cut short, by men with no thought, and no empathy
So what's left for our humanity?

When I started to write this, it was all about myself
How getting old has left me gathering dust on the shelf
And less opportunity leaves more time for contemplation
On how life's journey follows a natural progression
From selfish pursuit of personal glories
To a wiser understanding of other people's stories
Now I'm nervous of controversy, of the "political' angle
Because that world is so toxic, I don't want my words to tangle
While I balance on a tightrope
Across a chasm of no hope
But if there's one thing words can do it's kickstart a conversation
And that's what I'd like for me and you, that's my Theory of Evolution

So once more with feeling, bounce it off the ceiling, let it be healing:

Evolution, evolution, evolution.

AT THE ALTERNATIVE DISCO
GEORGE E HARRIS

In the deep den of red,
Trumpet basking cards on the table.
Escape to the other meter was un-sought.

Cavern spokes, narrow stairs and the tiny dance floor.
Avoiding the flailing fists of the posties out on a rave up.
Twenties was in town upstairs late 80s one day over
layered.

The fresh pull-out scented carpet comb.
Trembling waiting to enter with 50p door deductions.
Those hands were on course for a collision of mark ups.

Throwing shapes of seagull wraps,
Unearthing demons in cartoon zoom.
Walking back under fact of seeking unheard debris.

Days of wonder and we danced to the alternative sounds.
Energised seekers claiming they were there first,
But bringing in the extra sources as a matter of need.

The mixture percentage shakes at pressing beacons.
Darkened dew on creation slopes, striding to rare movements.
The hats now gone missing stolen in a swift action of laughter.

Peaking blisters and beating hearts of moons gone by.
Treble effecting, just bouncing into dark stars upon the midnight greens.
Rumbles talking loudly personalised bobbing on brink of falling.

One of the few alternatives that took place in the area,
Anticipations in sweat, sweeping the floor.
Ripped paper streams in clown flow, striking the deep dark dawns.

We are now in the afterglow blasting the effects.
Bands and sands on the rise we're still just listening into the radio.
Just got played in peel the morning its not yet struck.

Clocks go on I'm now thinking its not long.
Though millions of miles just now trans versing.
Memories of growing in those fractured shifts on the scene.

TUMBLR – ELIZA VEZEN

I know you don't remember that
But we've already met
Through the strange vines of the internet
On Tumblr, too! Don't fret
You were real charming In your black void turtleneck
I had black hair
And skin too fair
Not one percent of body fat
I was too young for that
But you liked the brat
In public you were very vocal
About the hatred towards patrilocal
About the patriarchal shit and all the nonces
But really
Did they ever tell you
You look exactly like that guy
Who married his adoptive child

HOW TO GRIEVE – KELLIE ADAMS

In no particular order
Scar your skin
Turn bone to gravestone
Bleed for the memories
Capture the fading

Put holes in your face
Become ornate
Decorate
the rage
Make steel armour

Cut your hair
Dye it
Become anew
Dispel disposable you

Eat your feelings
Starve yourself small
Take up more space
Take up no space at all

Become a doll
Be an alien
Make Latex a hiding place
Buy a cage

Date older men
Don't date
Practice celibacy
Perform

Do yoga
Lift weights
Learn Shibari
Get circus skills

Pretend the bath is womb
Float in utero
Light candles
Incessantly smudge

Count
Count days
Sheep
Hospital trips
Calories

Track
Track gains
Turnarounds
Recovery times

Cry
Have gratitude
Cry more
Give thanks
Cry more
Breathe

Allow yourself to be cracked open
Spill onto the floor
Stain the carpet
Definitely feel

Do all of this whilst time is weaving a net
Eventually, you'll transfer your grief there
You'll still have to carry it, but it'll be lighter.

PART OF THE ACT – SHEEMA HUQ

There'll be no wild
mishaps or random
wisecracks, and
vaguely mad quips
with crass gimmicks
and daft setbacks,
or crazy trials with
errors in stacks, or
bodged up lines,
while I lose all track,
as I'm scratching
my back with a
roofing axe. And I
won't be crying when
my jokes fall flat,
and I won't be dying
once I'm instantly
sacked, and If I'm
totally forgettable
the stage at least,
will be intact, and
while I'm utterly
terrible, my timing
shall be near exact!

Because boring them
silly is part of my act.

THE EMERALD – ODE BOY

An emerald glinting in the sun
Mesmerising
Fascinating, luxurious colour
From azure, through turquoise and bottle green
To jade and cobalt
Framed in black
Resplendent
Fit to grace any crown or aristocrat's hand in the land
Gazing deep into it's rain forest depths
It flickers with life
And then flies off to find another pile of dog****

CURIOUS, FURIOUS AND SORTED
FRANK MULLANE

Have you ever been furious about the source of your fast flowing river of tears
Did it move you to swim against the surging and crashing of decades of years
Or did you stay floating, coat-tailing the swell trying to make you unreal
Like an addict perfected, you weren't deflected, till you'd cut in the scars that won't heal

Can you recall in childhood when sometimes your choices weren't reaping buckets of gold
It's the same when your older when thinking the cards are way too enticing to fold
You can choose them for short term and spend a long lifetime lamenting that deal
Or you bravely discard them and find the soft presence surrounding the scars that don't heal

Now what can you do, its all up to self, to bring home the lessons gifted to you
You've really no choice, or you'll be dead in a month moving so quickly it's due
But you cannot get curious about the peace that's yours when blinding your eyes to a deal
And so you're missing, getting high on dismissing, the comfort around scars that won't heal

From YOURself to you, it takes mercy and love, so bleeding has time to stem
And BEE cos that's true, from now on you're higher than those seeking you lower than them
It's all coming back, not spurious nor fake, nor contrived, but happening for real
Allowing you time to set up to find the soft presence around scars that won't heal

A MOMENTS QUIET – MARTIN WROE

We take a moments quiet
Hold it, sit with it, eye it

We give it the once over
Scan it for signs of wonder

It seems a little reserved
We lack the time it deserves

If it's open to attraction
We're given to distraction

We settle for postponement
Return the quiet to the moment

AFTER YOU, I FOUND ME – MARIE RICHARDSON

Starting subtle, unfounded accusations
Dressed up and disguised as reasonable questions
Like 'where are you going?' 'Who are you with?'
The real meaning buried underneath.
Words of violence
Filling our uncomfortable silence
Two strangers occupying
The bed that we once made love in
The love turning sour
The wilting in the 'I'm sorry' flowers
But gestures fade, and you can't take back
The words you said when you felt under attack
And now you're gone
And I lie in that bed alone
Yet I've never felt more at home

This peace descending over me
So alien and yet so comforting
I'll build myself back up while wrapped in
Love from those friendships that really matter.
That you never managed to completely shatter

THE LINE – TONY COLLINGWOOD

There are thirty-four billion,
Six hundred and seven,
Dead people queuing,
To get into heaven.

Not the happiest sight,
For the newly deceased.
Stalled in a queue,
That their death just increased.

Yet they all shuffled forward,
A smile on each face.
For year after year,
In the light of God's grace.

And no-one pushed in,
Like bad people would.
And no-one complained,
Because they were good.

Then the clouds below parted,
For the billions to see,
That the line into Hell,
Was just thirty-three.

It took them a moment,
To process this sight.
Just thirty-three,
But - that can't be right?

How could it be,
That those who'd done wrong,
Had such a short wait,
Whilst theirs was so long?

They looked down at Hell,
With envious distain.
Like shoppers at Tesco's,
Who'd picked the wrong lane.

Then it took just the one,
Who could take it no more.
To break ranks with the good,
And head for Hell's door!

Like an ocean dam breaking,
The rest followed suit!
Billions of souls,
In selfish pursuit.

Down they all came,
This heavenly army.
Wave after wave,
A celestial tsunami.

They flew down as one, shouting,
"Hell do your worst!
We've waited too long,
The last shall be first!"

And there they arrived,
All sweaty with sin.
Ready for Hell,
To welcome them in.

But in the heat of the moment,
They hadn't thought though,
That their entry to Hell,
Was now stalled by a queue.

Then the clouds above parted,
For the billions to see,
That the line into Heaven,
Was now just thirty-three.

HER WILL – YASO BROWNE

Ungrateful was the weed
That I hadn't sprayed it yet due to the millipede
Weeks of work to claw through those cracks
How loud its green body visually tracks
This one seems to always flower
Beautiful ones too, a gentle power
I hesitate and think maybe just let it grow?
But a scan of the patio orders it to go.
Years of curation to abandon for guilt
Over something uninvited and designed to wilt
The sweet scent of the flower beds I planted
Remind me not to take order for granted
Spray spray spray and it shrivels
A pang in me says I was wrong to fiddle
I shake my head "this is madness"
How can I be the architect of this sadness?

PRESENT IN THE SHADE – Tom McDougall

Social commentating
Content creating
Activating
The Far right hating
Caught them the other day
Mass debating
About whether or not it's good
That dinghies coming over
Whilst they're deflating
Satanic holding
Scrolling
Trolling
People selling their souls
Of sex
For what?
A cheap money
On the internet
I've seen a lot of people in the gym
Trying to push away there problems
Not enough sets in the world
When their problems got a hold of them
Modern times
When kids on the estate
Have to duck and dive
From getting stabbed up by knives
People's perfect 5 minutes lives
Spruced up lies
Capture your eyes
Make you feel like you're not alive
or living

My mind
Is the toughest prison
I've ever been in
No reinforced bolts on a door
Can ever compare
To the chains shackled
Around my cortex's core

I know my way of thinking
Is sometimes flawed
I'm smart
I'm good at giving advice
But to it, I always ignore
Always wanting more and more
Trying to keep up with what
Mr jones has bought next door
One more magnet
for the fridge freezer front door
Another holiday album posted
online for sure
Remember no two people
Feel pain the same
And no one notices your tears
When you walking in the rain

My mind always works against me
Because when I'm meant to be doing something
But I'm always looking for the next thing

Any more I don't dream of being happy
But what I do want